Baby

Grassland

Animals

Jane Katirgis

Bailey Books
an imprint of
Enslow Publishers, Inc.
40 Industrial Road
Box 398
Berkeley Heights, NJ 07922
USA

http://www.enslow.com

Bailey Books, an imprint of Enslow Publishers, Inc.

Library of Congress Cataloging-in-Publication Data

Katirgis, Jane.
 Baby grassland animals / Jane Katirgis.
   p. cm. — (All about baby animals)
 Includes bibliographical references and index.
 Summary: "Introduces simple concepts about grassland animals using short sentences
and repetition of words"—Provided by publisher.
 ISBN 978-0-7660-3793-9
 1. Grassland animals—Infancy—Juvenile literature. I. Title.
 QL115.3.K38 2011
 591.74—dc22

                               2010011890

Paperback ISBN: 978-1-59845-156-6

Printed in the United States of America

052010 Lake Book Manufacturing, Inc., Melrose Park, IL

10 9 8 7 6 5 4 3 2 1

To Our Readers: We have done our best to make sure all Internet Addresses in this book
were active and appropriate when we went to press. However, the author and the publisher
have no control over and assume no liability for the material available on those Internet
sites or on other Web sites they may link to. Any comments or suggestions can be sent by
e-mail to comments@enslow.com or to the address on the back cover.

♻ Enslow Publishers, Inc., is committed to printing our books on recycled paper. The
paper in every book contains 10% to 30% post-consumer waste (PCW). The cover board
on the outside of each book contains 100% PCW. Our goal is to do our part to help young
people and the environment too!

Photo Credits: iStockphoto.com: © David Gomez, pp. 6, 12, © Graeme Purdy, p. 4,
© Jerome Skiba, p. 10; Shutterstock.com, pp. 1, 3, 8, 14, 16, 18, 20, 22.

Cover Photo: Shutterstock.com

Note to Parents and Teachers

Help pre-readers get a jumpstart on reading. These lively stories introduce simple concepts
with repetition of words and short simple sentences. Photos and illustrations fill the pages
with color and effectively enhance the text. Free Educator Guides are available for this
series at www.enslow.com. Search for the *All About Baby Animals* series name.

Contents

Words to Know 3

Story 5

Read More 24

Web Sites 24

Index 24

Words to Know

family

grass

In the grass, what do you see?

I see a baby.

I see a baby.

I see a baby.

I see a baby.

I see a baby.

Read More

Baillie, Marilyn. *Small Wonders: Baby Animals of the Wild.* Toronto: Maple Tree Press, 2006.

Kalman, Bobbie, and Sjonger, Rebecca. *A Savanna Habitat.* New York: Crabtree, 2007.

Web Sites

Enchanted Learning. *Grassland Animals.*
<http://www.enchantedlearning.com>
Click on "Biomes." Then click on "Grassland."

National Geographic. *Animals.*
<http://animals.nationalgeographic.com>
Click on "Animal Photos."

Index

family, 23
grass, 5, 21

Guided Reading Level: **B**
Guided Reading Leveling System is based on the guidelines recommended by Fountas and Pinnell.

Word Count: 46

I see a family.

In the grass,
what do you see?

I see a baby.

I see a baby.